Jackie Robinson

A LIFE OF COURAGE

Jackie Robinson

A LIFE OF COURAGE

by Keith Brandt

illustrated by Marcy Ramsey

Troll Associates

Library of Congress Cataloging-in-Publication Data

Brandt, Keith, (date)
    Jackie Robinson: a life of courage / by Keith Brandt;
illustrated by Marcy Ramsey.
       p.   cm.
    Summary: A biography of the first black baseball player to be
accepted by a major league team.
     ISBN 0-8167-2505-5 (lib. bdg.)   ISBN 0-8167-2506-3 (pbk.)
     1. Robinson, Jackie, 1919-1972—Juvenile literature. 2. Baseball
players—United States—Biography—Juvenile literature.
[1. Robinson, Jackie, 1919-1972. 2. Baseball players. 3. Afro
-Americans—Biography.] I. Ramsey, Marcy Dunn, ill. II. Title.
GV865.R6B73 1992
796.357'092—dc20
[B]   91-17852

Jackie Robinson

A LIFE OF COURAGE

The pitcher reared back and threw. The baseball whizzed toward home plate. But it wasn't heading anywhere near the catcher's mitt. It was aimed directly at the head of the batter, Jackie Robinson. Jackie jumped out of the way and went sprawling in the dirt. Then he stood right back up and got ready for the next pitch. It curved over the plate and Robinson doubled sharply down the left-field line. The crowd cheered, and his teammates joined in.

The year was 1947. Jackie Robinson, first baseman for the Brooklyn Dodgers, was the first and only black player in the major leagues. That made him the target of hate and bigotry in and out of the sport. Hotels closed their doors to him. Fans at every rival ballpark screamed ugly words at him. Even some of his own teammates were cruel to him. Worst of all, certain pitchers always threw at his head. But Jackie never backed down.

Jackie had a cool explanation for standing his ground. He said it was part of his strategy. "After you have ducked away from a close one, you can expect a curve ball." And he jumped on those curve balls every time.

DODGERS CLUBHOUSE

KEEP OUT

But there was more to it than that. Robinson wasn't just using his brains to get base hits. He was also being brave. You have to be when a 95-mile-an-hour fastball is coming right at you. Robinson wasn't about to let anyone drive him away from the major leagues just because of the color of his skin. He wasn't going to be defeated!

In the early years of the twentieth century, life was very hard for black Americans. This was true all over the United States, but especially in the southern states. It was more than fifty years after the end of the Civil War, yet black people still suffered.

Mallie and Jerry Robinson lived in a wooden shack near Cairo, Georgia. They were not slaves as their parents had been. But their lives were hardly any better. They lived in a house owned by a white farmer named Jim Sasser. They farmed a section of his land. They paid him for the land they worked and the house they lived in.

The Robinsons also had to buy things from Sasser. The seeds they planted, the feed they gave their chickens, their clothing, tools, and whatever else they needed came from Sasser's general store. By the time they paid Sasser for everything, there was little left for the Robinsons.

Every year was a 365-day struggle for Mallie and Jerry Robinson. Just to feed their children was a problem. Worst of all, it was a life without hope. The laws of Georgia said they could not own land. There were separate schools for blacks— schools without books, without heat, sometimes without trained teachers. Black people had no civil rights, and they were not allowed to vote. The Robinsons may not have been slaves, but they were not free in any real way.

On the evening of January 31, 1919, the Robinsons' fifth child was born. They named him Jack Roosevelt Robinson. He had three brothers—Edgar, Frank, and Mack—and a sister named Willa Mae. Jackie was a bright-eyed, strong baby, and a joy to his parents. But he was also another mouth to feed in a household that was already on the edge of starvation.

The strain of trying to survive became too much for Mr. Robinson to handle. He left, never to return. Mrs. Robinson knew she and the children had to leave the farm soon.

At that time, Mrs. Robinson's brother, Frank, came to visit. After learning what had happened, he said, "Georgia is no place for your kids. Come out to California. Things are better there. You'll have me and you'll have other kinfolk, too. It's a chance for a better life. You owe it to that happy little baby. Give Jackie a better world to grow up in. Give him a chance to become somebody."

To Mrs. Robinson, Georgia was home. The thought of leaving frightened her. Only the promise of a real future for her children gave her the courage she needed.

Over the next six months Mrs. Robinson did everything she had to to make the long trip. She sold the chickens, her few pieces of furniture, and every bit of clothing the family could spare. She even sold her pots, pans, and dishes. Every penny went into a jar marked "California."

By the spring of 1920, the Robinsons had enough money to pay for the train tickets to California. The cross-country trip took almost a week. The six of them rode in a section of the train marked "COLORED ONLY." The seats were wooden, and sitting on them day after day and night after night hurt a lot.

COLORED ONLY

Mrs. Robinson had no money to buy food during the trip. On the day before they left Georgia, she packed sandwiches and some cakes. "We have to make this food last," she told her children. "There will be no more till we get to California. So we'll do the best we can and not make a fuss about anything."

It was a long trip across the country. The Robinsons were met by relatives at the railroad station in Pasadena, California. Along with Frank were Mrs. Robinson's half-brother, Burton McGriff, and his wife, Mary Lou. It was wonderful to get off the train at last, and to see smiling, friendly faces. Mrs. Robinson had faith that this was the beginning of a better life for all of them.

The McGriffs lived in an apartment with three rooms and a kitchen. Even before the Robinsons arrived, the apartment was crowded. The McGriffs already had four children and a cousin living with them. With the Robinsons, there were thirteen people squeezed into those three rooms.

The crowded apartment had other problems. There was no hot water. There was a tin tub in the kitchen for washing dishes. The same tub was used for bathing. There was no electricity. An old-fashioned oil lamp was the only source of light besides sunshine. Food was cooked on a wood-burning stove.

At first, cooking wasn't a problem for the Robinsons. They had no money to buy food. The children's diet was mainly stale bread the local baker gave to them, and water with sugar mixed in. The McGriffs offered to share their food, but Mrs. Robinson was too proud to accept.

Things got a little better when Mrs. Robinson found jobs as a domestic servant. She cleaned houses, and washed and ironed clothing for families in Pasadena. Mrs. Robinson didn't earn much money, but the work had other good points. The clothing outgrown by children of these families was sometimes passed on to the Robinson youngsters.

As Jackie Robinson later wrote, "Sometimes there were only two meals a day, and some days we wouldn't have eaten at all if it hadn't been for the leftovers my mother was able to bring home from her jobs."

Mrs. Robinson had her own system of child care. Each of her children was responsible for the next younger child. Only Jackie, the youngest, was not expected to look after anyone else. Despite all their problems, the Robinsons were a close, loving family. The children stood up for each other, and the bigger ones protected the smaller ones. Jackie, the baby of the house, was surrounded by love and protection.

Mrs. Robinson was grateful to the McGriffs for taking in her family. But she felt it was unfair to take too much from the McGriffs. So she saved every penny possible. At last, with her small savings and help from the Pasadena Welfare Department, Mrs. Robinson was able to buy a house.

The Robinsons' new home wasn't grand, but it was large enough for them. There was a porch in front and a small front yard. There was a back yard, too, with room to play and grow a vegetable garden.

Moving-in day was as happy as could be. Mrs. Robinson sang as the children chased each other upstairs and downstairs through the rooms. Jackie, who was still a toddler, giggled and tried to keep up with everybody.

There was just one thing wrong. The neighbors didn't like having a black family living among them. These bad feelings lasted many years.

One incident burned itself into Jackie's memory forever. When he was eight years old, his mother sent him out to sweep the sidewalk. A little girl across the street started shouting, "Nigger, nigger, nigger!"

Jackie was hurt. He shouted back, "You're nothing but a cracker!" He thought that was a very insulting word to say to a white person.

22

The little girl's father rushed out of the house. He reached down, picked up a stone, and threw it at Jackie. Jackie dropped his broom, picked up the stone, and threw it back at the man. The stone-throwing went on for a few minutes. Finally the girl's mother came out and pulled her husband inside. Jackie heard her say it was crazy for a grown man to get into a fight with a child.

As a black American, Mrs. Robinson faced bigotry all the time. It hurt her deeply, but she refused to lower herself to the level of her attackers.

As an adult, Jackie Robinson wrote, "My mother taught us to respect ourselves and to demand respect from others.... My mother never lost her composure. She didn't allow us to go out of our way to antagonize the whites, and she still made it perfectly clear to us and to them that she was not at all afraid of them and that she had no intention of allowing them to mistreat us."

Jackie learned another important lesson as a child. That was to take care of himself. When Willa Mae entered kindergarten at the Grover Cleveland School, there was nobody at home to take care of little Jackie. So Mrs. Robinson sent Jackie to school with his sister. Miss Haney, the teacher, objected and sent a note home to Mrs. Robinson. It said Jackie must not come to school with Willa Mae.

The next morning, Mrs. Robinson went to see Miss Haney. "If I have to stay home to watch Jackie, I can't work," Mrs. Robinson said. "If I can't work, we'll have to go on welfare. I have too much pride to do that. I want to work!"

Then Mrs. Robinson asked that Jackie be allowed to play in the sandbox right outside the classroom. "He's a mighty good boy," she said. "He'll play there without bothering anyone."

Miss Haney admired Mrs. Robinson's pride and determination. She agreed to the unusual request. Every day the little boy sat in the sandbox and played all by himself. Sometimes Jackie was lonely. But he knew that it was important for him to be very good and to be quiet.

One morning it started to rain. Miss Haney looked out the window and saw Jackie sitting in the sandbox. His shirt was soaking wet, but he did not complain or cry. The teacher hurried outside, took the little boy by the hand, and led him into the classroom.

Jackie behaved so well that Miss Haney was very impressed. She praised him and asked Willa Mae to tell her mother what a wonderful child he was. From then on, Jackie was invited inside anytime it rained. He was also included whenever the class had a party.

Jackie's behavior was the first sign that he had a special strength. Somehow Jackie Robinson was able to deal with a tough situation and come out a winner. He won the respect of Miss Haney and the whole class. He helped his mother solve a real problem and he saw how it pleased her.

Jackie felt lucky to have Miss Haney as his own teacher when he entered kindergarten. He never forgot her. "She judged me as an individual," he wrote many years later, "and not by the color of my skin. She inspired me to believe that my chances for equal treatment from others were as good as anyone else's, provided that I applied myself to the task at hand."

Young Jackie was a hard-working student and he got good grades. But his finest efforts were at sports. While he was at Grover Cleveland School, Jackie recalled, "I told my mother to save money by not fixing lunch for me. The other kids brought me sandwiches and dimes for the movies so they could play on my team. You might say I turned pro at an early age.

"I discovered that in one sector of life in southern California I was free to compete with whites on equal terms—in sports. I played soccer on my fourth-grade team against sixth-graders who were two or three years older than I. Soon I was competing in other sports against opponents of every size, shape, and color.... The more I played the better I became—in softball, hardball, football, basketball, tennis, table tennis, any kind of game with a ball. I played hard and always to win!"

A close childhood friend remembered Jackie's speed and concentration. One of the games they played was dodge ball. A dodge-ball game has two teams. One team forms a wide circle around the other team. Players on the outside team try to hit players on the inside team with a large ball. Players on the inside team dodge this way and that to avoid being hit. When a player is hit, he is out of the game. The winner is the last kid inside the circle. When Jackie was on the inside team, he was always the winner. As his friend said, "The game finally had to stop because nobody could hit Jackie."

Jackie had more than natural athletic ability going for him. Edgar, Frank, Mack, and Willa Mae were also fine athletes, and they all loved to coach young Jackie. The Robinsons were the most athletic family in the neighborhood. They played football, baseball, soccer, and field hockey. At school they all ran track.

Jackie always played with the big kids. His brother, Mack, felt this did Jackie a lot of good. The youngest Robinson wasn't as large or as strong as his older teammates. But he was fast and smart. He had to be to get into their games.

When Jackie Robinson grew up he became a star with the Brooklyn Dodgers. His speed and quick reflexes on the base paths made him one of the best base-runners in the major leagues. He averaged twenty stolen bases a year over his career. No pitcher relaxed when Jackie was on base.

Young Jackie went from Grover Cleveland School to George Washington Junior High School and then to Muir Technical High School. Wherever he went, he was the No. 1 athlete. In high school he won letters in baseball, football, track, and basketball. Jackie's greatness was known all over Pasadena.

Before every game against Muir—in any sport—the other team's battle cry was "Stop Robinson!" But as hard as they tried, they couldn't. Some opponents tried to knock him out of the game physically. Other players tried insulting him. Their weapon was prejudice.

Jackie was called things that insulted his color, his family, anything that might hurt him. The players wanted to get him angry enough to lose his concentration and control. Jackie knew what they were trying to do, and he closed his ears to everything they said.

Jackie was still in high school in 1936 when the name of Robinson became known around the world. But it wasn't Jackie who became famous— it was his big brother Mack. Jackie's brother was a member of the United States Olympic track team. Mack won a silver medal in the 200-meter dash in Berlin, Germany. He was barely edged out by his legendary teammate, Jesse Owens.

Jackie was really proud of his brother. Mack was a winner, and Jackie vowed he was going to be one, too. At Pasadena Junior College, Jackie followed in his brother's footsteps. Pasadena Junior College wasn't known as a sports powerhouse. Then the Robinsons arrived. First there was Mack. Then came Jackie. Between them they put the school on the national sports pages.

In 1939, Jackie finished junior college and entered the University of California at Los Angeles. He planned to become a high school teacher and coach after graduation. At UCLA he was an athletic superstar. Even so, Jackie never considered becoming a professional athlete. In those days, blacks were not welcome in the major leagues in any sport.

Pasadena Wins Again
Thanks to Robinson!

Jackie Robinson left college during his senior year. He had to go to work. Mrs. Robinson needed his help with the family expenses. That was good enough reason for him to leave behind the cheers of the fans for a full-time job. Soon after that, World War Two began, and Jackie entered the U.S. Army. In time he became Lieutenant Robinson and was made morale officer for a black unit. After his discharge, in November, 1944, Jackie had to decide what to do with his life.

Jackie was offered a job as basketball coach at Sam Houston College, an all-black school in Texas. He was about to take it when, in April, 1945, he received an offer to play shortstop with the Kansas City Monarchs of the Negro Leagues.

In those days, there were separate leagues for
black and white baseball players. The Monarchs
were one of the best teams in the Negro Leagues.
Jackie took the job. It paid four hundred dollars
a month. That wasn't much money, but it was a
chance to play baseball—and get paid for it.

That same year, Jackie Robinson met Branch Rickey, the general manager of baseball's Brooklyn Dodgers. It was a meeting that changed Jackie's life and the history of American sports. The two men got along very well.

Branch Rickey had a daring dream: to wipe out racism in baseball. The first step to make that dream come true was to hire an exceptional black player. That great player also had to have the strength not to fall apart or lose his temper when bigoted fans and players insulted him. It didn't take long for Rickey to see that Jackie Robinson was that man.

On October 23, 1945, Jackie Robinson signed a contract with the Brooklyn Dodgers organization. Rickey assigned him to the Montreal Royals, one step below the major leagues. Jackie played second base for the Royals in 1946. That season he led the league in batting, with a .349 average, fielding, with a .985 average, and scoring, with 113 runs. He also stole forty bases. But even more important, he led the league in self-control. Branch Rickey knew Jackie was ready to take the next big step.

On April 10, 1947, the newspapers carried this announcement: "The Brooklyn Dodgers today purchased the contract of Jack Roosevelt Robinson, from the Montreal Royals. He will report immediately."

For the next ten years, Jackie Robinson starred for the Brooklyn Dodgers. His first season was tough. A few of his Dodger teammates refused to play with him. Players on other teams tried to spike him, and some pitchers threw fastballs at his head. But Number 42 refused to break. He answered back by playing baseball the best he could. And his best was great!

Jackie Robinson's baseball statistics are outstanding. His career batting average was .311. He led the National League in stolen bases in 1947 and 1949. Playing second base, he was voted Most Valuable Player in 1949, when he led the league in batting. Jackie retired in 1956. In 1962 he was inducted into baseball's Hall of Fame.

By 1972, when Jackie Robinson died, it was not unusual to see a black player in a major-league uniform. And it is not unusual today to see black professionals in *every* sport. But Jackie Robinson's legacy is even more valuable than that. His bravery and pride changed the way blacks are treated in and out of sports. Most important, it changed the way many blacks look at themselves. As the great Martin Luther King, Jr. said, "You will never know how easy it was for me because of Jackie Robinson."